A Tribute to Madness and Smiles

A Memoir of Bipolar II Disorder and Bulimia

AMANDA SZUMOWSKI

authorHOUSE

AuthorHouse™
1663 Liberty Drive
Bloomington, IN 47403
www.authorhouse.com
Phone: 1-800-839-8640

©2010 Amanda Szumowski. All rights reserved.

No part of this book may be reproduced, stored in a retrieval system, or transmitted by any means without the written permission of the author.

First published by AuthorHouse 7/27/2010

ISBN: 978-1-4520-5161-1 (e)
ISBN: 978-1-4520-5160-4 (sc)
ISBN: 978-1-4520-5159-8 (hc)

Library of Congress Control Number: 2010910634

Printed in the United States of America

Because of the dynamic nature of the Internet, any Web addresses or links contained in this book may have changed since publication and may no longer be valid. The views expressed in this work are solely those of the author and do not necessarily reflect the views of the publisher, and the publisher hereby disclaims any responsibility for them.

For all the people who never leave my side:
may your hearts never grow weary and your hands be held high.

Some names have been changed to protect the privacy of select individuals.

Life with bipolar II disorder and borderline personality disorder is a nightmare. In fact, living with this disease has been the complete polar opposite of the life that I keep dreaming and endlessly wishing for. My own personal reality is now a ghastly nightmare that I find myself aching and screaming to awake from. My illness is comparable to a demon, or some fictional devil that the world tells us is living among us. Maybe that devil is my illness, your illness, the world's illness, but who really knows. All I can tell you is that bipolar is devilish and fierce, raging and angry. It has crept its way deep into the halls of my mind and has twisted and contorted my brain into something that is unrecognizable to me now. It has reigned over me for years, and I have finally succumbed wholly to its evil.

My life has been a yo-yo of moods, emotions, and behaviors. The first palpable symptom of my illness was my eating disorder, which is what most of this memoir is about. Life with an eating disorder is not what you dream of the first day you decide that today is the day you won't put anything into this body of yours. It is not what you envision in the beginning. You suddenly find yourself slaved over the toilet bowl or locking yourself from the kitchen and crying yourself to sleep. What happened to all the "wow, you look great" compliments and all of the days you felt so high you could walk on water with that hollow stomach of yours. What happens is you find yourself curled up in a ball in the corner of a room somewhere, wishing this eating disorder away. You find yourself in a living nightmare and see yourself screaming for help in a room full of nothingness. You can't get rid of the pain anymore when you starve or when you vomit—the pain continues to get worse until you can't handle it anymore. You start to slice your beautiful, clean skin to purge the pain another way. The blood releases for a short time, but it is never enough. Nothing is ever enough. At the end of your rope, you look for the ultimate release, something that food, drugs, razors, sex, or money can't bring you. You find release in suicide, and you try to kill yourself.

I am twenty years old this year, and I have lived my life like this for almost eight years now. My life has felt like a never-ending vacuum that has sucked me deeper and deeper into despair and darkness, catapulting me into a living hell. Each year I become more ill, and I become more and more tired of living like this, but for reasons that are unknown to me, I can't get myself out of this pit.

I am writing this to talk to the people out there who struggle with mental illness. Whatever or whoever it may be—I am writing to you. My intent is not to tell my story but to tell you how I felt, in an effort to help you understand that you are not alone in this world, and there are people everywhere who suffer right alongside you. Our worlds become desolate and dark once we fully entrench ourselves in the throes of our illnesses. We become our illness; it becomes our identity. Our sickness is an overwhelming force and at times feels impossible to override. Although mental illness is powerful and demanding, the force and strength that we bring together when we hold hands and fight back is so great and so distinct that no other power can overcome it. We have to lean on each other through this—lean on our peers, our mentors, our treatment providers, our families, our friends. Lean on all of those who fight back with us, for someday we will join them on the other side. This is a tribute—a tribute to our madness and their smiles.

CHAPTER ONE

The sun had woken me from a deep sleep that cool summer morning on the shores of Old Orchard Beach, Maine. The smell of the sweet summer sun crept into my room, and I opened the blinds to flood the hotel room with the rush of cheery brightness that summer blesses the world with. That morning remains in my memory so clearly that it could have happened yesterday and it would have made perfect sense. The memory of my yearly family vacation is indeed my fondest, and I hold onto it when times and emotions become too heavy to bear.

Perhaps the most beloved memory of all is the feeling of the sand in Old Orchard Beach early in the morning once they have just brushed it through. The sand is so fluffy that it slides through your hands without friction of any kind.

My childhood could be considered a fairytale to most. I can't sit here and complain about parents who were alcoholics who fought all night long or being stricken by poverty and unable to get out of the living hell that it creates. My life was nothing like that. In fact, I grew up happy until I ran into the devil on earth.

CHAPTER TWO

Do you know what it is like to be raped? Do you know the feeling of having your legs spread wide open by force? Do you know what it feels like to have your face smashed by a clenched fist and hear "Shut the fuck up, slut, don't make a sound"? No, many of you don't, but sadly, many of you probably do. It is the worst pain. Yes, the physical aspect of rape is painful and damaging, but the emotional aspect is far worse. Your body becomes something unrecognizable to you after you are raped; it becomes like a rodent that you are pestering out of your house— and that house is your very own flesh and blood. Goddamn, it is the most annoying sensation you can imagine. When you take a shower and look down, you want to cut your eyes out with the razor blade placed next to you on the ledge. You can't even bear the sight of the violation that you endured. You can't put your hands on the places someone took from you. You can't bear it, you just can't fucking take it.

I felt that way for almost a year after I was raped. I starved myself so thin that I could no longer feel the flesh that he beat with his fists. I starved myself so thin that I couldn't recognize my body anymore, and my God, what sweet relief that was. I didn't want to put anything into this body of mine. I just wanted it to be fucking gone.

I went on with my outside life as well as I could: I kept going to my classes, and I kept smiling for all the family when I came home. But let me tell you, inside I was fucking living a nightmare. When my roommates and I went out on the weekends, I was terrified of men, but for reasons that I cannot understand, I was drawn to them. I searched every party for a guy that I could mack on and maybe find someone who could replace the memories of a man touching me. I was convinced that I could find a way out of this hell through meaningless hookups and sexual encounters. I could erase it. Between not eating, using drugs, and having sex, I could erase what he had done to me. Each weekend that passed I drank more and more and wasted away into nothing by the time April came around. I started slitting my wrists then—because nothing was fucking working. I couldn't get this feeling out of me, the feeling of wanting to erase myself and start over. The blood that ran down my forearms felt so good—the warm, bright red pain was releasing me for a time, and I could breathe again. It wasn't just one cut—it was four or five at a time. I needed to see mass release; I needed to get this fucking memory *out* of me. I sat alone in my room day after day, night after night, crying, pleading to God to let me please feel better. I stopped going to classes—I was so exhausted from the throwing up and the lack of food that I simply could not get out of my bunk bed in that crowded little dorm room.

It is almost exactly a year later, and I feel the same way now that I felt then: I just want an out. But let me start at the beginning of all of this. That is the only way this will all make sense to you.

CHAPTER THREE

Aside from my extended family, there was Lyndsay. Lyndsay was the woman who babysat me in my young years. I grew incredibly attached to her and flourished in her home as the years passed by. I still remember the smell of Lyndsay's house and the way her salt-and-pepper-colored hair was always thrown back into a ponytail. I remember the sound of the television in the afternoon playing *As the World Turns* and the way that her house felt like an entirely different world and dimension from my own. It is as if it was a great release to go to her house. It was almost like an escape from my own reality into a place that was always new and changing right before my eyes.

Every morning Lyndsay would ask me what type of doughnut I had for breakfast on the way there, and to my astonishment, she would guess correctly every time. I was amazed by her ability to predict (not realizing that at six years old, I had sprinkles stuck in the corners of my mouth), and I found Lyndsay to be so mysterious and wonderful. I also remember very clearly her sons Chuck and Scott, who were teenagers during the years I spent with Lyndsay.

They were constantly in and out of the house, going here and going there, and I can remember making up elaborate stories in my head about where Scott and Chuck were actually going. I imagined Scott was a secret agent who worked for all of the good guys in the world, ridding this awful place of all the bad guys that I knew of. I looked up to those boys with awe and wonder as I watched them mature and succeed during the years I spent with them. They were charismatic and hilarious, always picking me up by my tiny, delicate hands and swinging me around as I watched the world spin around me. The days of the week I spent at that house were my favorite days of all. Most of my fondest childhood memories involve that house.

As I reached school age, I entered another new world. School was supposed to be this fun and exciting catapult into independence and creativity. My personal vision of school was a place where kids went in on an assembly line, received lessons drilled into their heads, and then returned home to their real lives and real worlds. Obviously, when I started kindergarten, I learned something quite different. I was a well-behaved girl at school and excelled academically in my young years. I had quite a few friends at my elementary school and quickly became close to a girl named Samantha. For a short time, Samantha lived just a few houses down from my own, until she moved into a nearby neighborhood. Nevertheless, we remained best friends through her move to the new neighborhood and a new school. Sam and I were inseparable for many endless summers and remained that way until almost the sixth grade. Actually, when I go through pictures of my childhood, I can rest assured that in every other picture Sam and I will be playing together and sharing bouts of stomach-wrenching laughter. I adored Sam and the friendship we had. In fact, I can actually say that she was one of the few people in my life whom I had a genuine love for. My memories of our childhood are close to my heart, filled with playing basketball and playing with dolls, followed by evenings of bike riding and sleepovers in the late summer heat. My heart remembers all of the laughter we shared riding the streets of her neighborhood on our bikes, feeling so free and enthusiastic. I remember riding with each other up to the biggest hill of the neighborhood and flying down with no hands on the handlebars, hair plastered back in the wind, and smiling all the way down. It has been ages since I have felt so carefree and daring. Memories of feeling such strong, positive emotions provoke a smile and a giggle as I write about this. Our relationship was a central focus of my young life, and I valued our friendship immensely, but just as seasons change, so do friendships.

Sam was always a petite girl: small and beautiful with her cloudy blue eyes and her silky brown hair. I, on the other hand, was not petite as a child. I was always the taller girl, the one with the thicker arms and the rounder face. I was actually quite chubby as a kid. I never cared much about my body until I began to notice that others noticed the physical difference between Sam and me. Sam had a younger sister, Sydney, who was mentally challenged. I loved Syd—I thought she was blast to be around—but I kept that hidden in my own little head. Naturally, being older and "wiser," Sam and I excluded Sydney from most of our playtime. It was really a cruel thing. I remember an interaction with Sydney on one particular day; it was the day that shaped many of my years to come.

I was dropped off at Sam's house for the afternoon, and Sydney was playing in the front yard, rolling her hands through the mud. She then decided to make my brand-new white shirt her personal canvas and smeared handprints all over the front of it. Obviously, I needed a new shirt to wear, and Sam brought me upstairs to offer me one of her own. I tried to find a shirt, one goddamn shirt that would fit me, but none of them did, as my body was slightly rounder and thicker than Sam's. Okay, not slightly—it was significantly larger. The next thing I knew, Sam said to me, "Well, maybe you just need to eat healthy and lose some weight." That was it. There it was— the start of a long chain of self-destructive events that led me to the place that I am today. Now granted, Sam had no idea what she said would ultimately affect me so negatively, but that sentence was the foundation of a long and disastrous illness. From that very moment I knew there was something wrong with my body. The rest of my childhood was a snowball of negative emotions and thoughts flying in and out of my head at rapid speed. I began to heavily compare myself to Sam and to all the other children in my life and decided in my young mind that I was not even on a comparable level to them. Now I knew why my mother would only make the macaroni and cheese with half the cheese, and I found out why my dietary needs were watched so closely. I was fat. Oh my God, I was fat! My life became consumed with comparison, and I tried to pretend for every second of every day that I was someone else. I began to try to act like Sam for the day, thinking of what she would wear and what she would say. I thought if I became enough like her, I wouldn't hate myself so fucking much. Nothing seemed to work, as I grew and Sam stayed about the same size. With every passing year, I became less hopeful that I would ever be like everyone else.

I woke up every morning with the hope that I would like myself that day, or at least be somewhat satisfied with my performance for a decent amount of time. I lost touch with my individuality as a young girl, and it wouldn't be until ten years later that I would try to begin to find it again.

CHAPTER FOUR

2007

I was never tiny. Even at five foot four inches and ninety-five pounds, I was not tiny. Thin enough to lose my period? Yes. Thin enough for a weakened heartbeat, hardly palpable vital signs, papery thin bruising skin, and that bone-chilling cold? Yes. But it was never thin enough. I was never good enough.

I wasn't a functioning human being at this point. Between Prozac for my depressed and deserted moods and antipsychotics to keep me grounded in this strange realm of reality, I was constantly tumbling through my own mind, trying to discern what was real and what was true. Middle school and high school were hell, but I lived up to the part everyone wanted me to. I was so put together on the outside and so fucking bruised internally.

I believed beauty would come from thin. If only I looked as frail as I was, as broken as I felt inside, then maybe somehow the pain would be released. I achieved those delicate collarbones, structured by prominent bony shoulders. I lost the color in my cheeks, and my eyes faded to gray. I was finally as sick externally as I felt internally, but I screamed and I cried when I looked in the mirror, and I realized I was just as miserable as I was when I had begun.

How can such a sullen girl become anything of any substance? I wondered. I was trapped in my mind; I couldn't escape. I was alone, and I wanted to be left that way, forever.

Downward spirals were my specialty. Work too much, sleep too little, and eat nothing.

Oops, the floor is against my face. The parents are all watching from the side of the pool. Straighten up, Amanda, smile sweetly. It's nothing really. I must drink too many of those energy things. They don't work anymore; I'm too crazy, and I'm still tumbling.

I was so at odds with myself that I hardly noticed the pounds falling off like clothing on my thighs. I was so cold, so bone-numbing cold, despite the fact that it was July.

Then I experienced a relinquishing of control, an odd buzzing peace. My face grew fuller, my breasts softer. Was this health? This strange white noise when I shoveled food into my mouth?

I came out of that hospital, and I was a blank slate, something whole and new. Re-created and original. But returning home was only returning to the girl I had no desire to be. It would be the death of me.

In a sad attempt to regain control, I lost ten pounds. I was colder than ever, anemic teeth chattering. But still, I could not hold my desire for perfection at bay. When home becomes a prison, we must reinvent a safe haven. A nervous, skinny little thing, I feared emotion; I could not handle any relationships. Maybe that was what I was running away from.

Anxiety came back. *Disgusting little girl. Are you not embarrassed to be seen like this?* Another day, another breakdown. Another semester failed, this time before Johntmas. Drowning my sorrows in edible delights, I almost forgot how disgusting I was. My heart sat silent in my newly bulimic stomach, sleeping for now.

Health, oh how I wanted to know you. I even began going to the gym, trying to strengthen this now soft, delicate frame. But how evasive health can be. Perhaps it is easier to stumble upon than to actively pursue.

I never thought I would end up needing medical attention for something of my own doing. I would have happily dealt myself death, everlasting peace. But what can you do when you aren't the dealer? My heart was barely beating anymore; I couldn't even feel it when I reached for a pulse. Maybe I was dead, maybe I was dreaming. How did I go from being an angelic girl to something so raw and dissected that was too painful to even look at? My soul left me, and I was a corpse looking for life again. So much for everlasting peace. My life had fallen from under me, and the shattered glass of my remains had pierced my soul for eternity. It was just a waiting game now.

Somehow, in those short few years of my young life, I lost my identity, and I feared that I would never be able to grasp it once again.

CHAPTER FIVE

1999

My illness went with me wherever I went. When I was younger, I imagined that it would be released from me if I prayed hard enough: if I were a good girl, it would all be fine. When I got older, I got emotional. When I got emotional, I shut down, and my eating disorder turned on. I ran from it for years and years. I didn't want any part of it. I wanted to be normal—whatever normal is depicted as. Eventually it caught up with me, dismantled me, and turned me into a girl with distressing, aching green eyes but the most alluring smile you can imagine. It fooled everyone else, but it never fooled me, not once. I hated myself. I hated everything about myself. I spent my childhood years wishing day in and day out that I could be like someone else. From the age of eight, eight years old, a time when you are supposed to be obsessed with Barbie and playing house, I remember obsessing over everything I did wrong. I played Barbie wrong, I dressed wrong, and I was too fat, too ugly. I was too this, I was too that. In my mind I was one step behind everyone and everything else in my life. Nothing was ever just how I wanted it; I was never satisfied with myself. There are glimpses of happiness throughout my childhood, moments in time where I found myself suspended in happiness. But those moments play through my memory like the shattered glass of a mirror. They are whole and perfect and beautiful for some time, but when broken, it is impossible to regain every piece and replace it exactly as it was. I cannot retain memories like most people. I remember nothing about how I felt, but I always, always remember slight and vivid details. Details such as how a hotel room smelled, how many times you had to turn the lock on the outside of the door, or the way the sun would shine through the curtains in the morning. Nothing ever evoked feeling, but my detached and translucent memories are my only treasure.

Most of the memoirs written include a detailed life account from childhood to the present day. I guess I am different; I am breaking the rule of great works. I simply cannot recall my childhood in a cohesive state at this point in my life, and God knows, I am not waiting until the day that I can. I fear that day will never come for me; the day where I can make sense of my life seems so far from me that I cannot begin to imagine what it would look like, or worse, what it would feel like. I will tell you what I do know about myself, and I will tell you how I came to know it. I will tell you what has shaped me, what has given me life and taken it back again, what has made me and what has destroyed me, what has become the life that I know, the life that I long to escape from and the girl I have become, whom I cannot flee from.

CHAPTER SIX

At age ten I became a part of something that I never saw coming. It was something that I had only heard about in the media, seeing the horror on people's faces, or read about in novels that were light years beyond my maturity level. I became part of a trauma in a family that would tear them apart for years. At age ten I thought the only thing wrong with the world was my own physical being, that I was the route of my own unhappiness, and essentially only I could make myself such a miserable shot at life.

I was sitting on my aunt's couch one afternoon in the early fall, watching the leaves blow in funnel formations across the grass, which was burned from the late August sun. It was a red couch, well worn with the imprints of my cousins and their friends. It smelled of them, and it felt like them; it was a familiar place to me. My aunt's house had become one of my favorite places in my young life. It was the place I spent time with my cousin Natalie Rose, who meant more to me than anything in my tiny world. It was the place we had family dinners, where my parents laughed and conversed and I forgot about how miserable I was for some time.

Amanda Szumowski

My memories of that house are still so fresh to me. I can still smell my aunt's meatloaf cooking, and I can still remember the happiness I once felt there when my cousin would come walking in the door in the early evening after babysitting at the house next door. Her face would light up my afternoon. I spent hours upon hours playing with Natalie, whom I admired and adored so greatly. Those hours were filled with laughter and magical fairies, Barbie and Ken, and special secrets only the two of us knew. Natalie was five years older than me, and I worshiped the ground she walked on. She was so beautiful with her long, flowing dark hair and her delicate smile. I believed that Natalie had all the answers, that she was wiser than me, and that my world was okay when I was with her. I can still remember how she would show me the way through the pine trees in her side yard or how she would swim under my tube and pretend she was a shark in the hot summer months. I still remember the laughter and the smiles, the grass stains and the peanut butter sandwiches. I remember Natalie this way, even though by the time I was ten, years had passed by, and she was a teenager, focused on boys and makeup instead of dolls and dress up. Even still, Natalie was my universe, and I now had an intense fascination with young adulthood, simply because she was in the throes of her teenage years. I watched with eager eyes as Natalie matured and became more womanlike every day. I waited with great anticipation for the day I would become just like my cousin.

Then, just like a natural disaster wipes away life in nothing more than a split second, all of my happiness slid out from under me, and I was caught in the middle of something I could not begin to explain. As I sat on that couch, doing my math homework and waiting for my cousin to come home, I felt something was wrong;

I knew something had changed. I went upstairs to the bathroom and stumbled upon a moment in time I will never forget, a moment when I realized love can falter, and the essence of trust is something you cannot rely on. My aunt was on the floor of my cousin's bedroom, screaming in the phone receiver at my uncle, saying she never wanted him to come home again, she never wanted to see him again, she hated him, and she wished herself dead. I looked at her, sitting there on the floor covered in tears and black mascara, and knew at that exact moment that life could fall apart in a matter of seconds and you would never see it coming. The bedroom door was slammed in my face, and I scattered into the bathroom a few yards away. I slid to the floor behind a locked door and cried, not even knowing the magnitude of what was unfolding before my eyes that afternoon. I cried because I was alone and I longed for Natalie to come home to make everything okay.

Kathy, the best friend of my older cousin Sarah, was there that afternoon. At first I thought she came to offer support and love for whatever was happening to my aunt, but I quickly learned what had taken place after I heard them discussing the events in a locked bedroom while I had my ear on the ground to hear under the crack of Natalie's door. Tears rolled down my cheeks as I heard the words flow out of Kathy's mouth like the devil's tongue. My uncle, my godfather, whom I loved and trusted, had violated her. He had ruined this family, and he had ruined my trust in those I loved. I moved back to the red couch, back into the familiar indentations of my family's bodies, and hid behind my schoolbooks. I pretended like I had no idea what was taking place when Melissa came down to give me a hug good-bye, and I looked at her with such disgust when she walked out the front door. How could this girl live with herself? How could she just walk over here and blurt out such vulgar secrets and leave? How could this be happening?

I sat there in the same position for the remainder of the afternoon, waiting for my mother to pick me up, and it was that very afternoon in a house where I had once felt warmth and love that I lost trust in the world and felt nothing anymore but bitter air piercing my lungs with each breath. No longer did I hate just myself; I had found something else that was flawed, something else that I had to find anguish in.

Looking back now almost ten years later, I try to remember how I actually felt about what happened that day. Feeling, you know, expressing some sort of emotional response in reaction to an event. I don't remember crying after that day or even feeling heartbroken for my aunt or for her family like everyone else around me did. I was just watching from the inside out. I felt nothing besides a big black hole where my heart should have been aching with pain for the destruction of a family. Instead, I went to school, did my work, hated myself some more, and put that memory far away in the back of my little box, far enough where I couldn't touch it if I had tried. It may have been that my family was famous for ignoring elephants in the room and sweeping obvious, important events under the rug, or it may have been more of a defense mechanism for me. Regardless, I buried that day deep in the dark corners of my mind.

Elementary school progressed as it normally does, with parent-teacher conferences, field days, and picnics. I had joined a Girl Scout troop in third grade and spent most of my free time with my troop. I never actually enjoyed Girl Scouts. It was boring and time-consuming, and I had more important things to work on in the halls of my mind. It was all just a big comparison game to me. Who could get this badge or that badge, who could make the best birdhouse, who could get the most awards by each stupid awards ceremony? Of course, I never said that I hated it this much, because it gave me a place to belong—a place where I had friends. There was a girl who entered my life right around this age who shifted my focus almost automatically from attempting to mimic Sam to attempting to embody her. Her name was Alexandra, and she fascinated me. She was individual and confident and had a tiny gymnast frame that I longed for year after year. I quickly befriended her and began my mental obsession with trying to be just like her. I changed what I wore, and I changed my group of friends. I changed what music I liked and what movies I watched. I changed my entire world to fit into what I thought would make me happy. I started gymnastics and fucking sucked at it. I was clumsy and chubby and was never made to do back handsprings on a fucking balance beam. But regardless, I tried. The rest of my elementary days were spent trying to impress the three girls that I hung out with and trying anything that would release me from the body that I felt suffocated inside of. At the end of fifth grade, Alexandra moved away, and I lost a major source of my identity. I had to start middle school with a hole in my self-esteem and self-worth, which left me scared, alone, and dreading the next three years.

CHAPTER SEVEN

Everything in my life was so implausible from the outside looking in, but goddamn, my adolescent head was spinning with nothing but self-hatred by now. I fucking hated being myself, living inside of this body and walking around on this earth. Why was I blessed with parents who cherished me and provided for me when I couldn't even get up the strength to appreciate it? Why was I blessed with a beautiful roof over my head, all the things I had ever wanted, and an environment where a person could bloom and grow with each new day? Why was I allowed to live this way when all I wanted to do was slither away into darkness? What the fuck was my life coming to? Who did I think I was, just taking everything for granted, not seizing any good memories, and walking around like a corpse with no soul? Why was everything so put together on the outside while I was screaming from within?

I had two very good friends at this point; their names will remain unspoken. The three of us had a great time together throughout middle school and high school, with the "normal" ups and downs of high school friendships as they go. My life looked picture perfect, but in my own secret little world, I was the girl who envied everyone else. I envied my best friend for her tiny, little body and her bright blue eyes that attracted everyone to her, but I envied her mostly for her happiness and her carefree demeanor. I tried to act like her and mirror everything she did; I tried to love life like she did. I jotted down mental notes all day long in my head about how she laughed at this, she cried at that, and she found pleasure in something so simple. And meanwhile, I would think to myself, here I am, same old me. Fuck. Okay, so I was good at the flute, I was average on the swim team, I seemed to enjoy my life, and I seemed to be very personable and make friends easily, but I knew deep down what I was. I knew that I was dying to be anyone else but me. I knew every morning I would wake up and tell myself that today would be the day that I acted like I wanted to act. But in reality, I was a fake. A big fat fucking fake.

I think I was a junior in high school when I realized that I needed to do something about this internal nuclear bomb that was ticking inside me. I decided on what I hated most about myself and that I was going to fix it. Asking myself what I disliked most was so easy it was actually frightening. I was disgusted with my body, and I hated it more than anything. If I was thin, this time-ticking explosion would end, and I would be just like everyone else. I knew nothing about eating disorders at this point. I had no idea what being an anorexic or a suffering bulimic was. I simply decided that I needed to get thin and beautiful, and it needed to be fast. I stopped going to lunch in the cafeteria with my "friends." I use quote marks because I really secretly liked none of them. Instead, once I got my license at sixteen, I drove around for a half hour and chugged water and got a large black coffee from Dunkin' Doughnuts. I would go to class, sit, and not pay attention to anything but how good the girl next to me looked and how my thighs touched the fucking ends of those little wooden square seats and hers fell at least two inches short of that. I went to swim practice, sucked big time because, um, I was eating nothing. I would have an apple or a Gatorade during the middle of practice and jump back in to swim the pounds off my body. I had even convinced myself that if I was thinner and ate less, I would be a better swimmer, because I would have less body fat to carry in the water. I mean, all the star swimmers were thin, so my fucking fat ass would be too. So I swam until I could barely move.

Once I was in high school, I began to realize how good I actually had it. There were countless people in my school who were poverty stricken or troubled by a terrible family life. I, on the other hand, had a great home life and was given everything I asked for. I was mortified at the realization of my selfish lifestyle and convinced myself that I was not worthy of such love and devotion from my parents because I took everything for granted, walking around hating a life that many would die for. I believe this only added to the pile of self-hatred that I had been building for years and made me more miserable with every passing day.

I had joined the Manchester High School swim team as a freshman with my best friend alongside me. I knew that getting involved with something was the best way to attack the terror of my freshman year of school. I figured I would make friends and have a place where I was accepted rather than wandering the halls alone in my misery.

I made friends quickly with a girl named Megan, who was a junior that year. Megan took me under her wing and showed me the ropes of swim team and the way high school was. Megan was funny and charismatic, and in her I found someone to look up to and to be like. I felt honored to be the friend of a junior, an upperclassman. She and I began to confide in each other and quickly became best friends during my first year at MHS. Suddenly I was hanging out with a girl who had a car and had boyfriends, while my other friends walked everywhere and played Neopets. I was drawn to Megan's independence and slowly moved away from my freshman friends. Obviously, this caused tension and arguments between these two girls and me, but I didn't really give a shit anymore. I just wanted something new; I was tired of the same old scene. I obsessed myself with Megan and tried to forget that my life was still shitty even with her in it.

This book is about my life and all of my ups and downs, but I am choosing to leave out the insignificant parts. To some, it may seem absurd that I leave out my shoulder surgery and wearing a cast that made an upward right angle to school for six weeks. But to me there are bigger things that happened throughout my high school days—that stretched me to my limits— than my friendship with Megan or the unimportant other friendships that I made that first year. The big events were the ones that really fucked me up. One of which was my father's heart attack.

CHAPTER EIGHT

It was the day before my sixteenth birthday. In my little teenage fantasy world, it was huge. My sweet sixteen. Somehow, magically, I would turn into a beautiful young woman with the utmost grace and intelligence, and my past self-hatred would be left behind. I was having a huge party, with all my family and friends invited. I looked forward to it for months.

The day before I was actually happy and excited for once. I actually felt alive and *felt* happy. While I am feeling all of this wonderfulness, my father had a heart attack. He was setting up my massive tent for my massively overdone party, and what happens? A heart attack happens. I, being CPR certified and feeling like I knew everything that day, called 911 and determined precisely that he had a heart attack because I was demanding this extravagant party and it nearly killed him. The ambulance came, and I had to follow in my cousin's car, which wouldn't start with the door nearly falling off, and I remember thinking to myself, *Fuck you, Amanda; look at what you have done.* I am really nice to myself; I really value my self-worth and know that I am not the center of every terrible thing in this world. Ha, if I could only believe that, maybe I would have been okay.

Okay, so now everyone in my family was at the hospital all concerned about my father and his heart, and all I could think of was the fact that my party was not going to happen. Everything good in my life was ruined, and I was essentially the cause of it all. I caused my father's heart damage. I remember asking my mom if we were still going to have the party, and she promised me we would. And we did have that party. I look back at pictures of it, and I actually look happy at sixteen—well, from the outside anyway. I had long, thick, and beautiful hair and a perfect little pink sundress on, showing off my womanly shape. From the pictures, one would assume it was a day I was fond of in my memory, a day that came with happy memories and smiles. I remember it much differently, of course. I locked myself in the bathroom for ten minutes and bawled my fucking eyes out because I just wanted to feel like I looked, like on the outside. I was sick of pretending to be outgoing and loving; I was sick of being a successful young woman. I wanted to curl up in my bathroom and sit there until someone or something could come rescue me. My great-aunt knocking on the bathroom with an ear-piercing *"Hello"* initiated my rescue. I stood up, walked out, and blew the candles out on my fucking cake, wishing for a new soul.

CHAPTER NINE

All right, a little side note, skipping ahead about four years. I am working on writing this in my bedroom with my parents cleaning up dinner and my dog running around playing with toys. I am working on writing about how I remember my life, and my parents try and tell me that I am black and white, that my writing is black and white, and that I do not remember any of the good memories from my childhood. Awesome. I really enjoy reading something to someone and having commentary such as "No, you should have felt differently, you *were* happy, we swear." No, mom, no, dad, I was not *happy*. I am *still* not happy, and I am twenty now. My father makes some joke about how my mother was the cause of his heart attack, and they walk out of the room, leaving me here in my winter hat, sweatshirt that is ratty and way too short, and sweats. They leave me in here, pouring out my life, as they continue on with theirs.

I made it through my fifteenth year alive. My sixteenth year was a whole different ball game. At sixteen I suddenly felt that maybe someone else could make me happy. Since I had been living with myself for all of these years, maybe it was not me who could fix it, but someone else. Naturally, the idea of a boyfriend seeped into my head. Literally four days after my sixteenth birthday, I went camping with some distant family members (family members of the aunt and her husband who molested that girl). Wonderful people to surround myself with, huh? And literally ten minutes after the idea of a boyfriend passed into my mind, I met my first boyfriend.

He was a distant relative of these insane people, and he paid a good amount of attention to me that weekend. I got drunk one night with my "cousin" (not really, but I called her that) and lay out until the sun came up talking with her and this soon-to-be boyfriend of mine. I can swear to you from the minute I got out of the car at that campsite, and the minute that family saw his eyes on me, they had us married. I don't even remember feeling *any* sort of lust, joyfulness, butterflies, or whatever the fuck you're supposed to feel when you meet a boy you will fall in love with. I know I felt high, for the basic fact that I was high when I kissed him for the first time. Great first kiss it was, on a guardrail with some boy that meant nothing to me, so high that I tripped on my way to get to him, and he smelled. Awesome.

After that camping trip, I was suddenly hurled into a relationship with him. I know that I told him all the things you're supposed to tell a boy you meet and that I had a lot to do with the fact that we quickly became boyfriend and girlfriend, but I still have no idea why in God's name I chose him. I guess he made me feel pretty, as he told me I was the most gorgeous girl on the planet. That sure felt nice. Honestly, as I lie here trying to think back on our relationship, I can't remember our first date, I can't remember what happened at the end of that camping trip, I can't even remember how I got the title of being his girlfriend. My little self-hatred game took on a new form. It took the form of hurting myself through choosing horrible people to surround myself with and single-handedly ruining any sense of self-esteem my entire soul possessed.

I liked his family a lot; his dad made me laugh a great deal, and his mom had a very strong personality, which I was drawn to, obviously. His sister was a great girl as well, with dreams and goals and just a wonderful outgoing personality. I liked spending time there; it felt happy to me, and it felt safe. We dated for two years, my junior and senior year of high school. Throughout that time span, I became very, very ill. It is at this point where I can remember nothing about my relationship with him aside from little tidbits of trips he took, hanging out in his room, and other various unimportant aspects of our relationship. I do remember, however, being obsessed with making sure he called me at night, that he called me when I asked, that he texted me back within a thirty-second time period, and that I never went more than three hours without talking to him. I called him every morning to wake him up, and I talked to him every night before I went to bed. And if that didn't happen, I cried. I guess I can attribute that to my lack of self-worth and the obvious fact that I needed someone else to make me happy. I was extremely codependent on him and lost a big part of myself in that relationship (not that I had much to work with at the time anyway). I was still extremely obsessed with the fact that being thin would make me happy, because I was not having all of my needs met in this relationship I was in. He was not fixing my problem. He was actually making it worse, if that was even possible. I became very thin very suddenly my senior year of high school. It was right around the time that my relationship with my first "love" came to an end because he felt I was suffocating him. No surprise there—I was suffocating myself, and I was determined to bring someone else down with me. Now my life consisted of not eating, dealing with this mess of a breakup, handling the fact that we were still very closely tied via external family members, and trying to get into a fucking, goddamn college and pick a career. I fell apart my senior year; I literally went insane. I couldn't take it anymore. I was heartbroken over the loss of my relationship because now it was only me again. I only had myself to blame my unhappiness on, and all I could think was, *Fuck, what do I do now?* Everyone was asking me where I had applied to school, what I wanted to do, what my number-one choice was, and whether I could handle moving far away? My head was exploding with the pressure from the outside world, and my body was falling apart from the pressures of my internal world. And here entered anorexia.

As my social life began to melt away, my academic world fell right along with it. Through all of this mess and the turmoil going on in my world, I found a glimpse of hope in my high school anatomy teacher. She caught on to my game very early on, earlier than I think I even began to understand what was happening to myself. I grew rail thin in her class. I walked in day after day with black coffee, hyped-up on diet pills, looking like someone dancing on the edge of ultimate insanity. She asked me a few days in a row if I was okay, and I kept feeding her the line I fed everyone: "Yeah, I am fine, don't worry." Well frankly, no I was *not* fine. I was walking around my high school with nothing in my stomach, a spinning head from mental and physical exhaustion, and a broken heart. None of which is "fine." My entire world was not fine. I had no idea what I really wanted to do with my life, my friends were becoming more and more distant as they began to see me melt away to nothing, my family was worried, and I was living in a house full of tension and anguish. I remember thinking that I felt as if my brain would just rupture from the amount of overwhelming emotions I was housing. Actually, I wished that it just would.

I began to talk to my anatomy teacher on a daily basis about what was going on in my life. She was such a strong and positive influence on my life. She was a nurse and a fantastic, successful teacher, as well as an outstanding mentor to me. I found hope in her that someday I would become someone who could help, someone who could give back what I had taken from so many people, and someone who would triumph. I kept going to that class, even though I had basically given up on my others, and it was a damn good thing that I did.

I was severely addicted to diet pills my senior year. I was taking at least four times the recommended dosage of those toxic things. They caught up to me, as I had suspected they would, and I had to ask for help. I knew it was time for me to open my fucking mouth and spill. I'd had an episode of fainting my sophomore year of high school that was diagnosed as conversion disorder, more commonly known as bullshit. I knew it was the result of my eating disorder, and I didn't give a fuck at that point. I was still fat, and I needed to reach my goal. My life *needed* to be okay. But two years later, possibly from acquired wisdom of the eating disordered world that I was no longer physically okay.

I was lying in bed one school night during the late winter. I'd had nothing to eat for three days, and I was rewarding myself with an apple—how exciting and exhilarating a reward that was. As I lay there, I was planning out my next day and how I was going to avoid food at all costs. My chest began to hurt, and my heart raced. My palms became clammy, and I started to wonder if I was having an anxiety attack. I dismissed it as such and rolled over. After twenty minutes of that, I got scared and went upstairs. Now the act of actually going up to see my parents was an act of a higher power because I had absolutely no intention of asking for any sort of help from anyone, let alone them. Nevertheless, I dragged my freezing, frail body up those stairs and said, "Mom, help." I told them about the diet pills, and I told them what was going on that night. My chest stopped hurting at some point after our one AM conversation, and I crawled back into my bed, mortified and terrified. My secret was out, and it was not just mine anymore. I had passed it over to the two people who would actually make me do something about it. Fuck. Why the *fuck* would I do that. Well, because I didn't want to die.

I got up for school the next morning and felt fine. Again that word. I really fucking hate the word fine. It means nothing. Not one human being can actually say that he or she is fine at any given moment in time. You could be hungry, you could be tired, you could be happy, you could be sexually frustrated, and you could have no job. No one is fine; the world is not even fine, for Johnt's sake. But I guess if you can convince someone that you are indeed fine, the majority of the population will believe you.

I got my coffee, blasted Kate Nash, downed three Hydroxycuts, smoked my cigarette, and went to anatomy. Obviously, I had no concentration span anymore, and if you had walked into that class, you would have seen me taking my notes, looking at the board, and listening, but you would notice that I just looked up and down at the board and at my paper. I had no emotional reaction to anything anymore, and every physical reaction I had was delayed. I felt that rush of pain again in my chest, and I felt paralyzed from the sensation of a skipping heartbeat. I got up, asked to go to the bathroom, and hit my side on the desk on the way out. I remember thinking that if I could just get a little air I would be okay; I just needed to take a little walk around the lovely halls of my high school and the pain would diminish like it had last night. It didn't. I went back, sat down, and waited for the bell to ring, which seemed to take years at the time. When it did, I looked at my teacher and said, "I don't feel well."

Shortly after that day, my teacher contacted my parents, telling them how concerned she was and that I really needed help. I think I may have shed a tear when she called them. But I don't remember much about this time. My brain was literally like soup, and I have little memory of the events that followed that phone call. I know that I saw a therapist and nutritionist, but I can't even remember if it was before that day or after. Honestly, I would have to ask my parents. That's frightening. I had no feeling anymore. Everything just passed through me like I no longer existed. It was what I had longed for. I had got down to that weight that I believed was the magic number to my eternal happiness, I had pushed everyone out of my life, and I was still fucking miserable. I *still* hated myself. I gave in at that point, knowing that if I didn't reach out for the hand my parents and doctors were lending to me, I would not survive. So I grabbed it.

CHAPTER TEN

While everyone my age was preparing for graduation and getting ready to move on with their lives, I was in the hospital being fed Ensure and talking about my feelings. Feelings that I had wished away for years and that I was being forced to deal with as every drop of fucking food settled in my stomach. They watched me go to the bathroom, and my days consisted of eating, talking, eating, talking, going home, throwing up, and going to bed. Looking back, I could have used that program to my advantage, but I just didn't really give a fuck about it. I met some really unique people there, some people that I actually felt somewhat understood me, and if nothing else, I regained hope that there are people in the world worth letting in. The timing of everything was very shitty because it was right at the end of my senior year. I would be missing graduation, senior skip day, senior trip, prom, everything. Although I didn't care about all of that shit anyway, I still had a burning desire to be able to experience it. The first event was the senior trip.

I had to go late, having my mother drop me off with my little lunch box full of my dietary needs. I was excited to feel like someone normal after a month of IOP at an insane asylum. I had asked my two best friends at the time to meet me at the entrance so I wouldn't have to go through six hundred people to find them. When I got there, they were not there. For some reason, I will *never* forget how I felt at that moment. My heart sank, tears rolled down my face, and I went alone. Alone in a place full of laughing teenagers, deserted by my "best friends." I had to find them on my own, and when I did, it was not what I had in mind. I hadn't seen anyone in quite some time, and I expected somewhat of a warm welcome back. Instead I got, "Oh hey." Oh fucking hey. I hated that day; I still hate that day. I had looked forward to it for so long, and once again I was let down by the world. Clearly, I was in a "woe is me" frame of mind at eighteen, but I didn't fucking care. It was just one more excuse for me to find fault in myself—not only did I not like me, no one else did either. Cool. My life was really getting better.

You know, I should have slapped myself out of that when I was able to do so, before this became my entire life and before it became my identity. But you can't go back and change things, as much as I wish I could, and so it did become my life; it controlled me and everything that I did. I know that people reading this who either have had or are currently suffering from an eating disorder wish they could go back and slap the fuck out of themselves until they wake up and realize what they are getting into. It's more than just a clinical disorder; it's a big vacuum full of daggers taking pieces out of you as you get sucked further and further in. It took my high school life from me, it took some valuable relationships from me, it took my self-respect, it took my self-esteem, and it took the joy out of my eyes and the enthusiasm out of my life.

CHAPTER ELEVEN

How do I even begin to introduce the next chapter? How do I tell the story of a relationship where I thought I had found my soul mate but instead I found hopelessness and despair? I guess you start from the beginning, like we always do. We come from nothing, and we become something. I'm still looking for that something I am supposed to become. My second year of school at Sacred Heart University was terrible, to say the least. Between relationships that I wish I had never started and an eating disorder that was out of control, I began to lose my mind. Now, when people use the phrase "I'm losing my mind," it does no justice to the select few individuals in this world who really do lose it. Losing your mind is not a sudden event. It is a slow, lingering, and painful experience that seems to last forever. It's like submerging yourself in ice-cold water. First it stings, then you go numb, and finally you find yourself struggling for life with no way out. That pretty much sums up my sophomore year. And the kicker to the end of 2009 was this relationship I found myself in. Suddenly I found myself unable to breathe, move, and even speak. My home life became volatile, my love life was a pit of despair, and all I could think about was death. What a concept death was. It overtook my mind that winter; the blissfully simple act of removing your soul from a place of such misery was incredibly seductive to me. The unbearable depression that tore through me found a lifeline in suicide. I could never calm my mind down, and it ran ramped with morbid thoughts about how this world really would be better off without me. My mind flooded with negativity more and more each day, and I felt as if I was drowning in my own self-destructive thoughts. What a fucking concept.

I should have known that this relationship I was in was destined to fail. I knew this guy—or boy, I should say—in high school, and I absolutely hated him then. He was such a dirt bag, always thinking his words and actions never hurt anyone, or worse, not even caring. He thought he was cool because he had a lot of exterior and such fake, plastic friends. God, he actually embodied everything I hated about high school as I rerun the past like a film in my head. We really never had much interaction, expect for this dumb, fucking party that I went to at his house while I "dated" his friend Ben. I don't even remember what went on, but I know I caught him talking shit while I had gone to the bathroom, and some weird argument happened after that. Once again, my memory is so fogged with illness that I cannot even remember what made me hate him in the first place. I wish I could remember that night, or at least remember the hate I had for him. It might have saved me from total self-destruction. I never thought this boy would be one I fell in love with. Not in a million years. I wish I had some intuition; it would have been a great advantage at that point. But like many things I wish I had, I didn't.

And so, we begin.

CHAPTER TWELVE

My sophomore year of college was an absolute disaster. I was walking through a minefield at Sacred Heart. Everywhere I looked there was a ticking time bomb waiting to explode. I maintained my exterior, and I played the part of a stressed-out college nursing student who was tired, but making it. I tried to keep it together, I really did. But every day became harder and harder, and I was just giving in and giving up. I was living with the two girls that I had befriended my freshman year, and I was ecstatic to get the chance to live with them. They made me actually laugh and feel something besides miserable. I really thought my sophomore year would be completely different from any other year of my life. Then reality hit me smack in the face. My sophomore year became a drunken mess and a year full of loneliness, casual sex, drugs, and a total lack of self-control. It started out all right. My grades were actually really good, and I was happy living with the seven girls I lived with. I felt independent and grown-up for the first time, away from my parents and able to make most of my own decisions. Reality check—I should have never left sight of my parents. Going out once or twice a week and drinking with friends morphed more quickly than I could have imagined into me drinking alone, smoking pot alone, and losing my mind alone. I sat in my college dorm room and stared at the wall, thinking of all the ways my life was turning to shit, how I really couldn't muster up the courage to fix it, and how much I felt paralyzed in that very chair. How was I supposed to do anything if I was paralyzed? Even if I wasn't physically incapable of moving my body, my emotions were refusing to leave the corners of my mind and keeping me trapped in that chair month after month. My bingeing and purging became so severe that I was taking three showers a day, just so I could throw up. I walked down the stairs in my building and threw up in the bathroom on the first floor. I threw up in bags; I threw up in anything I could dispose of. It was disgusting. I hated every second of it, and I wanted to curl up in a ball of my digustingness and disappear. But that was impossible. So I kept on the same path, spending every day planning out when I could binge, where I could purge, and when I could use drugs. The purging went from twice a day to seven times a day in a matter of a few months. I was physically exhausted and still going to classes at this point. I stopped taking my Prozac, and within a week of that horrible decision, I was a black hole. I couldn't get out of bed, I couldn't put clothes on, and I couldn't live. Obviously, now being the therapy expert that I have become, I knew something had set this off. You don't just transform into a walking black hole without something happening to you in the real world. Looking back now, I can see exactly what set this explosion off, what sent me into this living hell. But at the time, I had no idea what was going on. I had no idea what I was doing to myself and what was happening to me.

I knew I was depressed and that my mind would never shut off, I knew I had an eating disorder, and I knew I was miserable. But I was so far gone that year that I could not even begin to face my reality. Actually, I simply did not want to.

On a side note: I am going to leave some pretty significant events out of this section. Or, perhaps the better term is, I am going to tiptoe around some things that happened to me in 2008/2009 for the sake of my own well-being and for the sake of the people who know and love me. This is not to say everyone in my life is left in the dark, as my therapist and nutritionist are well aware, as well as other professionals I have opened up to along the way. But sometimes things are better left unsaid. That was a hard lesson to learn.

CHAPTER THIRTEEN

So here we are, 2008. I was a complete disaster, physically and emotionally, the walking black hole of Sacred Heart University. My mind and my sense of self had been sucked into darkness, a never-ending vacuum. I felt nothing, I was numb to any emotion passing through my distorted mind, and I had no reaction to anything that happened to me that winter. I was now involved in a very risky sexual relationship with a man I had known for a few years. We never dated, never mentioned each other to anyone, and kept our relationship a big secret from the outside world. It was ours to hold onto, and it was all so fun and magnificent and mysterious while it lasted. I should have never been involved in *any* type of relationship at this time, never mind such a black-book sexual scandal. I came when he called, and I listened to his every command. My sense of self was gone, and I found comfort in the ability to please someone else. He made me feel beautiful, mystical, and important. All of his words flowed through my brain like water into a dehydrated body. Those words filled me up, kept me going for at least one more day, and made me feel that I was at least alive. I never took notice of his forcefulness when we slept together or how we always had to be loaded before we made it into the bed. I blocked out the nights when he yelled at me for not performing correctly and the nights when I got hit for being tired. None of this registered in my mind as a problem. I mean, I got punished if I wasn't meeting expectations. That is a part of life, isn't it? I never felt anything those nights; I just rolled over and went to sleep. It may have been because I was stoned out of my mind, or it may have been because my mind shut off to save me from such damaging events. Either way, I felt nothing. Even the day I had the shit beat out of me, I felt nothing. I went over there after he called me to come, knowing that he was drunk and angry for things I had done. I knew exactly what I was walking into. I drove in my car, blank-minded and numb, to a place where I was only going to be hurt. I got out, walked to the door, smiled, and got my face smashed against a wall. After a good ten minutes of fighting, he stopped. Picked me up and said, "Shh, it's going to be okay now, my love." He put me in the shower, washed the blood away, and fucked me. He fucked me so forcefully that I cried. I screamed actually. He was so drunk that I couldn't get through to him even if I tried. So I shut my bleeding mouth and closed my haunted eyes. The next few hours are a complete blur. I got kicked, slapped, screamed at, derailed, and degraded to nothing. At some point, he passed out, and I left. I got in my car, drove for an hour, climbed in the backseat, and smoked a bowl. I smoked until I saw nothing. I smoked until my reality was no longer in existence, and I went to sleep. You would think that I would have said something to my therapist about this event. But no, I kept my mouth shut. My philosophy was that if I kept my secrets to myself and I blocked them out of my mind, they weren't real. If I dared speak of them, they would become reality. And if that had become a reality to me when it was actually taking place, I probably would have killed myself. My every move after this was based on blocking it out, forgetting, numbing, anything. Anything that would take what happened away.

I went from party to party with my college roommates, trying to believe that I was actually happy to be in college and finally able to go out and party without questions being asked. I smoked pot, I drank jungle juice, I played countless games of beer pong, but I could not capture the essence of freedom that I thought college would bring to me. I was too busy worrying about how skinny I looked or if people actually liked me or if they were just pretending. I was convinced that my roommates thought I was insane and that secretly they wished they had never moved in with me. I didn't know why I had such self-hatred and low self-esteem, nor did I have any idea how I would ever get rid of it. I just kept going through with the motions, hoping and praying that I would eventually feel better.

I lived with seven other girls that year in a three-bedroom suite with one bathroom and the smallest kitchen known to mankind. I am a total neurotic neat freak, and living with three slobs in my house was like living in a torture chamber. Our apartment was constantly disgusting, and it drove me totally nuts after months of living there. I don't know why I was so obsessed with keeping a clean living environment, but I became enraged when I realized what a disgusting mess I was living in. Actually, when I think about it, I probably liked to keep everything so perfect and neat on the outside because my internal world was like World War Three.

Regardless of the reason, I fucking hated it. I grew to hate three of my roommates as well, as I learned what type of people they really were. It was just a complete disaster. One of my roommates had a pretty severe gambling problem, as well as numerous other issues. The other was the living example of what blond girls from California are like in real life: snotty, rude, and self-centered. The last one I didn't really hate, because I never talked to her much, but she was messy, and that was enough for me to decide that she was no good. I was obviously being harsh and judgmental, but I didn't really give a shit. I mean, really, I went to a school with the snottiest people on earth as the general population of the campus, so I had a right to become cold and foul as I attended the university. Aside from all of that nonsense, I found unexplainable love in the three roommates I did care about. Franci, Ashley, and Kristen quickly became the very best friends I could ask for. We laughed and laughed when we were all together, and I found people who were actually willing to listen to all of my assorted issues. To this day they are still my closest friends, and I am thankful for the chance to have lived with them and have shared so much time with them by my side. They were there through my sickest times that year, and although they never said much, I know they were concerned. It was written all over their faces every day. I wish I could have been more open instead of lying about my whereabouts and stealing food to binge and purge on all the time, but I was so suffocated by my eating disorder that I couldn't find my out. I made my amends to them while I was in Chicago, but I will never forgive myself for being such a deceitful friend during that time. I had no intentions of hurting them in the process, but I ended up getting them pretty pissed off at me after a while. I wish I could go back and change the way I acted—as I wish I could with the entirety of my life—but that is impossible. I love them, and I will never thank them enough for all that they have done.

It's no surprise that my life fell apart that year. Every normal person would have a meltdown after that. But I of course, having to take it to the next level, had a complete mental breakdown. I lost my mind in the late winter. I withered away to nothing. I stopped eating altogether. I slit my wrists wide open to try and see the pain released from me. I didn't feel pain from what had happened to me; I felt pain just from being me. I was trapped inside myself, and no matter how hard I tried, I was still fucking there. No amount of blood released the trapping sensation I felt. No amount of hunger, vomit, tears, drugs, love, hate, pain, fear, happiness—nothing could save me now. I was trapped and never coming out. I was screaming on the inside, and the thirty-four cuts on my wrists and inner arms were screams that I couldn't force out of my mouth; they were screams for help.

My screams were heard, and they were loud and clear to a woman who I was becoming closer and closer to as the weeks passed by. My nursing professor Eileen was the one I found myself taking refuge in as my life began to decompose. Eileen was my Foundations of Nursing professor during my sophomore year. She was this tiny person, with such a fire about her that you couldn't help but be enthralled by her personality. At first, she intimidated the shit out of me. I was already a nervous wreck going into my sophomore year, as I knew the course material was getting more serious and I really had to give this my all to make it here at Sacred Heart. I was so nervous that the first day of class I found myself sweating and shaking as we walked into the building. Then I met our professor, and I nearly passed out. I sat through that two hours thinking that there was no way I could talk to her about the fact that I would have to miss a few classes here and there for treatment. I was convinced that she would be so incredibly angry that she would kick me out of the class for making excuses on day one. Obviously, I am a very irrational person, but I literally sat there in fear the entire first day of classes that semester. Once the class was over and everyone had left, I approached her with my knees trembling, my hands drenched in sweat, and my voice cracking every third word. I have no idea why I was so incredibly nervous about telling her a basic fact of my life, but I was a basket case. So I basically told her the blueprint of my treatment and how I would need to miss a few classes that semester because of an eating disorder. To my surprise, she did not kick me out of the class and have steam coming from her ears, but she simply looked at me and said, "Okay, we will work this out together." Holy shit, I must have been dreaming. I had a stunned look on my face for about thirty seconds after she responded and just said, "Great." I walked out of the classroom and got into my car and smiled. Finally, there was someone who knew I just needed to hear the basic factual response that she gave me.

CHAPTER FOURTEEN

From that first day of classes, I fell in love with her as a professor. She was so honest and hilarious about all of the experiences she had to share from her years as a nurse. It was refreshing to have a professor who understood we didn't really want to be sitting there taking notes but rather we would all like to be in bed at eight AM. She made us feel as if we were understood, and in my opinion, that is the finest quality a college professor can have.

As the weeks passed by, my treatment was steadily declining. I was slowly giving in to the glorious eating disorder that warped my mind. As I gave in more and more each week, Eileen began to notice. She started pulling me aside after class, asking me if I was okay, and of course I assured her I was fine and went on my way. But as my face grew pale and my clothes grew larger, it was becoming harder and harder to fool the public. I was ecstatic to find out that she was assigned as my clinical instructor for second semester, but deep down I knew that my secret would soon be found out with her seeing me more often now. At this point, I was now visiting her office once a week to talk to her about what was going on with me. I started to let my guard down in her office, something that was extremely out of character for me. I had no idea what it was about her that made me feel comfortable enough to talk about what was actually going on in my life, but I did. I began to tell her about how hard it was becoming to keep up with all of my schoolwork and how dreadful I was beginning to feel physically. I would sit in her chair weak and pale, hands shaking from exhaustion and dehydration. She offered me such meaningful advice about how I would make a wonderful nurse but I had to take care of myself before I would be able to help anyone else. I knew she was right, and I tried to help myself that semester, but I was beyond my own help at that point. Shortly after we started our weekly meetings, our class began clinical. It was here that Eileen watched me fall to my knees. I remember her pulling me aside after we were done in the nursing home one day and telling me that she was worried. All I can remember thinking is I was worried too. I knew that I was in trouble now. I was throwing up at least four times a day, and I was forever in a state of delusion from the lack of food and hydration. My brain was becoming soup, and all I could do was stand next to myself and watch it happen. I was scared. The next few weeks were a mess of starvation and misery, laxatives and Diet Coke. I started to e-mail Eileen daily, and in all honesty, she was the only thing that kept me from falling to the ground. I promised her I would take one less laxative a day and eat a banana. She knew that my potassium was low long before it nearly killed me. It's important to mention here that I was seeing my therapist twice a week and was in group therapy with her as well. I love Cindy—she has been wonderful over the past few years—but our relationship is strictly professional, and I needed someone who was outside of my treatment world to enable me to see what I was doing to my life and myself. My nutritionist has been a blessing to me as well, and I have a fabulous relationship with her after two years. But again, she was inside my treatment world of eating disorder professionals, and I just couldn't get a grip on my reality through my doctors. They have both helped me tremendously in my recovery but only when I actively choose to use them to my advantage and put the effort into recovery. Clearly at this point in my life, I was not willing to use my resources. In DBT (dialectical behavioral therapy), we talk about willing versus willful as an extremely significant factor in the ability to recover. I was willful my sophomore year, meaning I had the idea I wanted to recover, but I had no willingness to actually pursue it. I continued to watch myself fall deeper and deeper in my illness, and the deeper I fell, the less hopeful I became that there was happiness beyond sickness.

In the meantime, I started talking to the boy from high school, the one to whom this chapter is dedicated. While my world was spinning out of control, I got a facebook message from this boy. We got to talking, he told me what a crush he had on me in high school, and I fucking fell right for it. Of course I did; I was so emotionally drained and weak that anyone who took a genuine interest in me I clung to. We talked and talked, spending hours on the phone. It really seemed like he had changed into a different person since high school, and I liked who he had become. We started to hang out, hook up, all the usual start offs to any relationship I have ever had. I remember sitting on my couch in my living room, lying on him, and he ran his fingers up and down my spine. I felt every touch on every bone. I remember thinking to myself, *shit*. His touch intoxicated and warmed me, while my bones were so cold to human emotion that my mind went haywire. I knew I felt something for him, something I hadn't felt in quite some time. His very presence made me joyful. Amid all of these feelings I remember thinking that I must *really* be losing it. Now I was despondent inside my own hell, with this delight seeping in through the cracks in my brain. It was like poison, and I sincerely felt like I was dying.

Well, in actuality, I was really dying. Less than two months into our young relationship, I was told that I needed to go to the emergency room immediately after a blood test came back. It was low potassium, the silent killer of bulimia. And so I found myself in my roommate's car, being driven home to parents, who were worried sick. I will never be able to repay all of the things my friends did for me that year, and I will never forget thinking to myself as my roommate drove me home, *how do I deserve a friend like this?*

So I sat in the hospital for three days having potassium pumped back into me. Still, I insisted on numbing. I would drag my IV into the bathroom with me and throw up anything I had eaten while I was there in that hospital. It was that weekend when I realized how unwell I really was. I was in the hospital from pretty severe complications from bulimia, yet I was still throwing up. It was this weekend when I learned that I would be going to Timberline Knolls in Chicago for residential treatment. I had to leave my new little boyfriend. I was forlorn.

He knew the reality of my situation from day one, and I told him that I was going to have to go away for a few months. He told me he would wait for me, and that we would talk every day. I got on a plane to Chicago and left everything on hold.

I will go into Chicago later, or perhaps somewhere down the road, when I get to the point in this book where I actually talk about recovery. For now, we will talk about two months later, when I came home.

CHAPTER FIFTEEN

I came home happy and healthy from Chicago. For the first time in my life, I was able to smile and feel it, cry and get back up again, say I love you and know it meant something. It was such bliss coming home like this. I came home and jumped straight into a relationship, which I was warned not to do, but I didn't care. I was in high spirits, and this guy was going to only make me happier. God, he did. The months flew by, and we did everything and anything together. I knew it was something. He actually cared about my issues, took interest in learning more about them, and asked me question after question. I felt such liveliness while around him that I could hardly contain myself. I felt like I was living finally. I felt like I wasn't trapped inside torment, and it felt so fucking good. I fell in love with him. I never thought I would fall in love again after my first boyfriend and after all of the recent events. But I fell in love with him. I remember lying on his couch, about to make love, and I said to him, "I want to say something, but I'm scared."

He said, "I guarantee you I'll agree with you." I told him I loved him, on his living room couch, in the freezing air-conditioned room, with the smell of summer all around us, and surrounded in his embrace. His words flooded my body with warmth as he said, "I love you too." Having sex with him was something so surreal to me. He was gentle and compassionate. He touched me softly, and he was content. I let my guard down with him; I was horrified of sex before him for obvious reasons. But regardless, I let him touch me, and he touched me with love, and his love restored me. His love brought existence back into my dreadfully eerie eyes.

We soon spent every night together. Each day I arose exuberant, knowing I had him by my side, pushing and combating this illness right along with me. We had our love, and it was stunning to me. It brought meaning to my life, and it slowly mended my heart back together. We did everything together; every free moment either of us had, we were side by side and hand in hand. He came to visit me at the salon I was working at often, always bringing my favorite coffee or a home-packed lunch on Saturdays. He wrote me love notes; he left little notes in my planner for school where he thought I wouldn't see them. He texted me all day long; he made me laugh even with his brainless, little, futile texts. He had me with my heart wide open to him. I visited him at work, I did artwork for him, and I left surprises at his house and notes on his car. We were in love ecstasy. He came to therapy with me, to learn how to assist and what works and what doesn't work with the psychologically ill. He embraced my past and took my might and ran with it. He was a constant reminder that there is happiness past illness. We were so in love, and I was certain that there was no one else in this world for me but him. We fell so in love in eight months that we talked about marriage; we talked about jobs and kids and a house. We got dressed up on Friday nights and went out pretending we had money to look at engagement rings. I tried them on while he had his hand on the back of my neck, rubbing it and telling me how striking the ring looked on my delicate hands. We said "I love you" at least a hundred times a day, and everything felt so perfectly in place. It all felt right. My life felt right when I was with him. Granted, I was so stressed out with school, work, and treatment that I had to drop a few classes and had to quit my job (which I now blame on my impulsivity). But still, my life felt tolerable because I was in love, and I saw my future in his perfect blue eyes while he wrapped me in his arms and told me it would all be okay. His words will never leave my head—the words that made me believe in love again, the words that made his love for me factual. I will never forget. They replay day in and day out. It was a hot summer, it was a wonderful summer, and it was a summer I will keep close to my heart forever. Summer turned to fall, and we fell more and more in love with each passing day. Our love seemed resilient, and I thought that I had found my soul mate, but once winter began to settle into the late fall air, I realized that holy fucking hell, was I wrong.

I got pregnant. This was the beginning of the end of our relationship. The two of us utterly freaked out, as any twenty-year-olds would. We did the right thing, or so he thought, and told our parents and began to try and assess what we were going to do. He had his mind made up. He would have it no other way but abortion. His parents also had their minds made up, although it was never their decision anyway. His mother was so comforting to me, promising me it was the right thing to do and that our love would make it through this. He told me that we would be married in two years, and we could have children then. He promised me a wonderful life, but only if I did things his way. I began to get pissed after two weeks of this and finally told him that I didn't know what I wanted. I was sick of having people's opinions shoved down my throat, and I needed to breathe. I was being suffocated, and I could not even see, never mind feel. I thought I wanted an abortion. At first, it seemed like the right thing to do. It was the practical thing, and it would benefit us both in the future. We went to the abortion clinic in Hartford, Connecticut, one Friday morning. It was our second time there, as my first test had come out negative because I was so early. This time it was for sure, and we planned to make an appointment to have this abortion. I went into the bathroom to pee in the disgusting little plastic cup that yields the result of life in your womb. While I was peeing and dreading this appointment, he knocked on the door and said, "Amanda, we have to go."

I got angry and yelled, "What the fuck, I'm trying to pee. Leave me alone."

He said, "There is a bomb threat in the building. We are being evacuated." Fucking *awesome*. Not only did I have to deal with the protesters on the corner, now I had to evacuate because someone was considering bombing the building I was in. What a grand morning that was. So he called his mom. (He was very dependent on his mother, which I had never noticed and sadly had to figure out this way). His mom told us to try somewhere else. She had no regard for the fact that it was somewhat disturbing to have to be evacuated from a place that you didn't even know if you agreed with. She just wanted this baby gone. She wanted her son to graduate from college, get a job, and be normal. This baby was not in her plan, and she insisted it be aborted. She insisted on it so much that I believe she manipulated her son into believing the same thing, though I will never be able to say for sure. Anyway, we drove to West Hartford and went to the Planned Parenthood there. It was dirty and disgusting, and the doctor was running late because he had heart trouble that morning. I walked the fuck out of there. I knew something wasn't right. Something was telling me this was not what I wanted, but rather what everyone else wanted. I cried in the car, and my boyfriend told me it would all work out, and that no matter what, he would always love me. I will never forget those words coming out of his mouth. I stared him dead in the eye and asked him, "Are you sure?" He assured me we were meant to be, and our love could outlast anything. I held those words close to my heart.

During the next few days, I packed up my stuff from his house, as I was staying there to try and figure things out and let my house calm down. His mother had been kind enough to offer me a place to stay, and I was and still am grateful for that. It gave us some time to spend together, though it was probably to my disadvantage in the long run, with their beliefs being thrown at me every thirty seconds. A few days went by, and I went to my therapist and then to family therapy with my parents. This day was the day I was going to make my final decision. I had informed my boyfriend that I was really uncertain of what I wanted, and that day I would choose, for sure. I talked it out, and I knew in my heart that I didn't believe that an abortion was the right choice for me. I knew that he would be mad, and that it would probably take him some time to come to terms with what reality was, but I never envisioned what was to come. I called him on the way home and told him I was keeping the baby. He hung up on me, and I pulled in my driveway. He called back as I walked into my house, and I picked up to him screaming. He told me I was sick and that I had no idea what I was doing. He told me this would be the last time I would ever talk to him and that he despised me. He told me he wanted no part of this, and he hung up the phone. I tried calling back but got no answer. So I called his house. His father picked up, and I asked him to please have his son call me when he could. His father told me that I would have no communication with him, and in the background I heard his mother say, "No, we are done." At the time I had no idea that I was currently in a relationship with my boyfriend *and* his mother. I had no idea that she controlled his every move and that I was in fact speaking to her when I spoke to him. What a frightening realization that was. This was the end of our relationship. My boyfriend left me. The boyfriend I just told you about, the one who had wanted to marry me twenty-four hours before this. He left me, and told me he didn't love me. He told me I was dead to him. Twenty minutes later, I fell apart. I fell to the floor in my bedroom and heaved for an hour. The person I wanted more than anything in this world had left me because I got pregnant. He left me to pick up the pieces of our relationship alone. I had put all my trust in the world in this boy (I refer to him as a boy because any *man* wouldn't do this), and I was heartbroken. I literally lost all optimism in the world that day. Here I was, pregnant and alone, and had no idea how I had gotten there. I tried calling him for days, tried to reach him somehow. Eventually, after he didn't pick up for two days, I went to his job. I walked in the gym where he "worked," if you can even call it that, and I walked up to him and he said, "You need to leave." That mother-fucking bastard. I told him I wanted two minutes of his time, and he motioned me to the door while he dialed his mother. I think I actually laughed at that. How fucking pitiable he was. So I screamed at him, started to cry, and threw the Coach wallet he had gotten me at him while I made an ass out of him at work. I walked out of the gym, and the two girls he worked with came up to me asking me if I was okay, which I obviously was not as I gasped for air. He came out and told me he was calling the cops on me. I went into shock at this point and just left. An hour later, an officer called me and told me that he didn't think that this boy was doing the right thing, but he had to do his job. I was astounded at the level of maturity my boyfriend lacked. It was actually distressing. Who the fuck calls the cops on his pregnant girlfriend who only wants to talk? The girlfriend he wanted to marry for eight months prior to this night. I remember thinking that I was in a dream because all of this was so surreal to me. What a fucking idiot.

A few nights ago, I wrote a letter to him. It is some therapeutic approach to moving on from someone who has hurt you. I personally think it's bogus, but I'm out of options at this point. And of course I have to include it in here. In all its rage and vulgarity, it is the truth. I feel strongly that he was very wrong, and I will never change my outlook on the subject. So here it is, here you go, bub.

CHAPTER SIXTEEN

You have destroyed me. I have let one person, one sick and mentally fucking retarded boy, devastate me. I loved you so much; all I wanted was a life with you. I saw my future in you. And you fucking claimed that you loved me? No, you asshole, you did not. All those things you said to me were lies. *All of them.* I am holding so much of this anger within me that I am exploding. My heart was fucking bulldozed when you called the fucking cops on me when I tried to come see you, less than twenty-four hours after you said you wanted to marry me. Fuck you, fuck that walk we took in the woods to try and figure things out. Fuck you for telling me that if I had an abortion, we would have kids in two years. Fuck you for trying to manipulate me into what you wanted me to do, and fuck you even *more* for telling *me* that I manipulated you. I was confused, and your fucking retarded parents were shoving their biased shithead opinion down my throat with every chance they got. How was I even supposed to breathe between you, them, my parents, and myself? How did you expect me to just give the fuck in to what your dumb fat ass wanted? Of course you wanted an abortion, you disgusting piece of shit. You wanted no responsibility, and everything you ever told me about how much you loved me was a complete bullshit lie out of your ass. *How do you think that made me feel?* When I finally realized that you were lying to me for eight months, that when we went out all dressed up pretending to be rich and important and looking at engagement rings, *it was all a big lie.* And I was so in love with you. How sad it is to think I loved such a boy. The damage that you have inflicted upon me is immeasurable, and it is something I will never forgive you for. You are a waste of life, and I feel sorry for whatever girl you end up with. I fucking hate you. All you are is one *big, fat* (literally) *liar.* And I hope you get what is coming for you somewhere down the road. And your mom? She can suck a fat one for all I care. She better be thankful that I didn't derail her at Target when I saw them and embarrass the fuck out of her while I had the chance. I should have reminded her that you were probably at home waiting for her to come so she could suck on your tiny pathetic excuse for a dick. (I always lied when you asked if it was big.) I know you probably missed her. And for you, Ms. Perfect, I fucking hate you just as much as I hate your fat, ugly son. What makes you think that your son is some prophecy that walks the earth, expecting everyone to just follow his will? I don't know what planet you are from, but maybe if your son had looked like Jude Law, then I would listen. But he doesn't, and his brain is the size of pretty much nothing. So fuck you for thinking that it is acceptable for your son to leave his girlfriend under such circumstances. Fuck you for making him drive with his father so that you could have time alone with me and make sure that I didn't try and warp his brain into thinking maybe he could try and think for himself. I should have driven off the road that night had I known better. You are a manipulative bitch. And if you dare call me manipulative, you need to take a look in the goddamn mirror. You have your husband on a chain at home, and frankly it's quite disturbing. No wonder your other son can't get out of bed in the morning. Shit, I would be depressed too if you were my mother. Fuck everything about you, fuck you for thinking that you know everything, and fuck you for thinking that you're better than me and that I don't know what is best for me. You are very blessed to still have your self-respect after I saw you at Target. I really could have let you have it, but I don't have the energy to waste on your pathetic existence. As I told your son, you should probably move away when he graduates, if that ever happens, because you can now sleep at night knowing the entire town of Manchester, Connecticut, knows what your family did to your son's girlfriend. Oh, and your cake tasted like shit. I lied so that you would like me. Oh, and on the subject of morals, where the fuck are yours? You think that it's okay for you to do what you did and I am to blame for the end of our relationship? No. Wrong. You are wrong, point blank. You were wrong, you are wrong, and you will always be wrong. So stop all the pretending like your household is some family portrait of the American life, because it's not. You have a morally bankrupt son who eats too much, a deadbeat who smokes pot in your garage, and a husband that isn't really even considered a man at all, because he has no voice in that house. You forgot how to teach your sons how to treat women, so I feel very bad for whomever they end up with. Actually, I just feel bad for you. You're pathetic. What a life. So fuck off, as I said before, and know that you are hated by me and I hold my head high while thinking back on what happened. Go have another cake and have a nice life, and make sure you wear ChapStick when you are around your son, you bitch.

And back to you, bub. Your family is revolting and should really consider moving somewhere after your dumb ass graduates from college, if you even do. Because rest assured, the town knows what you have done. I have taken care of that minor detail with great precision. *Fuck you.* I would rather have my *mental* issues than your moral issues. Go cry to your mom about all your woes and have a nice life. Be sure to warn your next girlfriend of your severe dependency on your mom. It's uncomfortable to find out the way I did. So for your own self-respect, be sure to forewarn. Good luck and *good-bye*, you morally bankrupt, fat moron with a small dick for such a large man. I hope you have a suitable life.

Love, Amanda.

That was probably the most honest and most vulgar thing that I have written in my life. God, it feels good to just be honest. That is the beauty of writing: you can just get it out, and there it is. Right there for you to see, your emotions and feelings out, on a clean piece of white paper. Now I realize that this letter will offend some, but I don't really care. If you don't like it, stop reading. My memoir is my memoir, and I am proud to write it just the way I would like. That is what my boyfriend did to me, and that is how strongly I feel, and I will never back down. Actually, it was fun writing it in my kitchen, reading it to my mom as I went along laughing. It is nice to know that when the pain is unbearable and you feel like you can't move one step farther, you can. Whether it is for ten minutes, or ten days, you will be able to move, and the pain will subside. Not to say it won't come back, but for that period of time that you are okay, get it out. Get out what you feel, like I just did. I am laughing at it now, but in twenty minutes, I'm sure I will be curled up in a ball in my bed missing him and what we once had. But at least I got it out. It's one less thorn that I have to pick out of my heart. One less three-hour crying marathon and one less cut on my body. For God's sake, get it the fuck out of you, whatever it is. It's freeing. I will publish this with that letter in it, regardless of what is deemed appropriate. It's from the heart, and that's what matters to me.

CHAPTER SEVENTEEN

So, it was a very interesting night last night after I wrote this. I had finished, shut my computer, took my cocktail of night medication, and got into bed. The amount of pills I take to sleep is outrageous, and they all make me very drowsy and completely out of it. I probably fell asleep around nine thirty and went into my nightly coma. Around two thirty, my dog got up, needing to go out. I tried to ignore her like I do every night, but I gave in and got up. I hit my cell phone to see what time it was, and I saw a text from John's phone number. *Jesus Johnt*, I thought. *You have got to be kidding me.* So I looked and it read, "Hope your holidays were good." Now, of course I gave in to him automatically. No matter how mad I get at him, I still miss him. And at this point, I don't have the strength to ignore him. So I asked him why the fuck he was wishing me a good holiday, and he told me it was because he was drunk. I had figured as much. Clearly I was not in the best frame of mind, totally conked out on my medications, while I texted him back. We went on and on about how we couldn't get over each other, how we missed each other, and how we each blame each other for our relationship's demise. His argument was that I fucked him over and broke his heart while ultimately destroying his ability to love. Oh, please. It's so pathetic. I just told him we will never see eye to eye, but it doesn't change how much I miss him. What I should have done is e-mailed him what I had written a few hours before instead of playing into the pity party we were having. He told me he has fucked like five girls, but he still thinks of me. None of this I believe, because he had only had sex with not even a handful of girls before me, and I *know* the girls in this town know better than to mess around with his dumb ass. Regardless, it still felt so good to talk to him. No matter how much I disagree with his actions, I cannot get over what we had and how goddamn good it was. Everywhere I go in my town, I think of him. Every second that goes by, I still think of him. Every song I hear, every book I read, everything. I am always reminded of him. My heart aches for his return, but my logical mind knows quite well that his return is something I will never witness.

After all of this turmoil and all of this heartache, I lost the baby. I started bleeding very early on. I thought it could just be a normal part of pregnancy. But as the weeks passed, the bleeding became increasingly worse. I scheduled appointment after appointment to try and figure out the cause of the bleeding, praying and begging God to not let this be a miscarriage. This baby was more than just an embryo to me. This baby embodied a chance at redemption and a chance at finding hope within my desolate world. This baby gave me the motivation to move forward with my life and the strength to get over John because it would be an unhealthy relationship for this life growing inside my womb. I found hope in my life where I thought hope would never come again. But after all of my praying and all of my dreamlike hoping, I found myself rushing back from my therapist's office to an emergency room. I sobbed all the way home, knowing exactly what was taking place as my body cramped and contracted. I walked into the emergency room, red-eyed and weak, and sat down in the intake chair. They asked me my name, and all I could get out of my mouth was "I'm pregnant, and I'm having a miscarriage." I closed my eyes and waited. I don't know what I was waiting for that night. Maybe I was waiting for someone to come and tell me it was all a big mistake and that my baby was fine and the bleeding was a figment of my distorted mind. Maybe I was waiting for John to come rushing in to save me. Maybe I was waiting for God to save me. All I know is I was waiting for something that was never coming, and waiting for something like that destroys a person. The nurse came in and placed my name band on and said to me, "Oh, you are a cutter? You know, honey, that leaves scars that will never fade." I looked at her straight gray hair in a bob cut clinging to her oily face and asked her to kindly shut up. Don't fucking tell me what cutting does. If you are not a cutter yourself, you are incapable of registering in your brain what the act of dragging a razor blade over clean skin does for the fragile mind. I lay in that hospital bed examining the scars on my arm; I was trying to remember what each cut represented. The first five on my left arm represented sadness; the first five on my right arm represented shame. The next eleven on my left arm represented pain, exhaustion, hopelessness, and fear. The next thirteen on my right arm represented repentance from sin. Thirty-four slices in my skin, thirty-four expressions that I could never purge from my mouth, so I had no choice but to purge them from my skin, the only other way out. As I looked at those scars, I could only cry. I knew all those emotions all too well, and they were written all over me. I did not know happy anymore, nor did I know patience, acceptance, tolerance, and love. I knew nothing but my own selfish pain. The nurse came in again, and I could only stare at her circular glasses and stringy hair and think, *What do you know about pain? Do you know the pain I am in or the pain the world is in? Do you see how pathetic our existence is on this earth that God created for us? The wars, the violence, the hate, and the sin. I mean, fuck, we are all doomed as it is, but does anyone else see this horrible suffering that I see?* All of a sudden a probe with a camera was being shoved up my vagina, and I snapped into reality and looked at the ultrasound screen. I did not see my baby anymore; all I saw was a disgusting and elaborate mess of a womb. All I could think of is that this picture I was staring at was an absolute identical image to my life. I started to panic then. My heart raced, and I just wanted to rip the camera out of me and run. I wanted to run from my life; I could not take it anymore. I wanted to run directly into nothing. I wanted to run into blackness and infinity. I wanted to forget my existence and float away into nowhere. But instead of running, I was sitting right there in that bed, covered in white sheets stained with the blood of my baby. The nurse gave me a Percocet, left, and came back with my discharge papers. She was telling me something about how I have to wait for my period until I can try and get pregnant again, but all I could hear was white noise. I heard nothing, I smelled nothing, and I saw nothing. I signed my name on a piece of paper, got changed, and walked out with the Friendly's Diet Coke my mom gave me. I walked to the car and called John's mom to tell her I'd had a miscarriage. I told her, I hung up, and I watched the world fly by me as my father drove me home. All I could think about was opening up the door and falling out into traffic. Maybe then I would find nothing.

CHAPTER EIGHTEEN

The days blended together. The cold, harsh winds of winter ripped at my skin, and I lay wrapped in my bed under my three comforters, trying to forget that I was alive. After two days of this, I decided I needed to get up and get on. I needed to get on with my life, do something, go somewhere, and be someone. The first step to this was obviously to get my nails done. I went to my favorite place in the mall, where the girls are all a mystery to me as they speak in Chinese to one another. They all look so happy, so vibrant, and so youthful. It thrilled me to watch them for a half an hour as they painted my little, fragile nails. I stood up, and I felt a rush of blood from below onto the pad that I was wearing. I thanked them and ran carefully to the bathroom in Panera Bread. I looked down, and I saw my baby—my product of conception right there in front of me. About the size of a chicken liver and covered in blood, the sac that once contained life looked like a massively large blot clot. I took my pad off, wrapped it in toilet paper, and threw it in the metal "female product" container hanging on the stall. I washed my hands, and I walked out. I got into my car and I drove. I drove with no music, no intention of going anywhere, and no intention of ever returning anywhere. I had just passed my baby, my little embryo, and threw it in a brown paper bag inside a metal container. I might as well have taken a sledgehammer and cracked my skull open. The pain was that real. I went into shock that afternoon. I completely shut down my brain and all electrical function my body possessed and walked into my room and sat on the floor. I don't remember what I thought or what I felt. I just remember shutting everything off and watching everything go black. The next few weeks were just a blur of darkness with people's supportive words swimming around in my head. I felt as if I had fallen into a hole that got deeper and deeper with each passing second, and the ladder that was left for me inched up higher and higher. I composed myself for the outside world to see, going to my therapy and trying to pretend that everything was okay when in fact, absolutely nothing was okay. I tried to tell myself that this was God's will, but I felt as if I had lost all faith now. I was so far from light and hope that I could no longer feel the warm touch of a higher power on my skin. The days were so excruciatingly long, and the nights were never long enough for me to withdraw into and remove myself from the world for some indefinite consecutive hours of darkness. I started to think that I deserved this blackness. I deserved to have nothing anymore. I deserved such torture. And so, I began to think about the ultimate and end-all solution to such misery, suicide.

 The weight that I felt upon my chest was so unbearable that I felt I could no longer manage to take one tiny pathetic breath. I drove down to my therapist, knowing that this was indeed something I needed to express to her. I needed to tell her I felt like a cinderblock was crushing my bones, and poison was seeping into my blood. But I could not verbalize such things to humanity. It sounded so dramatic and cliché that it made me want to vomit as I imagined myself sitting in her leather chair telling her just how bad I actually felt. I simply could not tell her this. I think during that session I managed to explain to her that I was tired of fighting and that I didn't want to do this anymore, but I came nowhere close to expressing the amount of pain I felt internally. I told my group that I felt hopeless and alone, but I looked at their faces and knew that there was something more written on my face and crawling out from under my skin. I left therapy and drove through my town that night, reminding myself of all the wonderful memories that were buried somewhere in the halls of my depressed mind. All of these places that I once had fond memories of had become nothing but desolate places of coldness and sorrow. I tried to force myself to remember laughing with my cousins, playing on the swings with friends, throwing snowballs back and forth with other children, anything, anything at all to provoke some sort of warm, happy feeling in my rigid freezing body. I felt nothing anymore about these places. I only felt numbness. So I drove home.

The following day I drove down to see Eileen. I had given her a bouquet of flowers the day before for being such a wonderful and positive influence on my life, and I was actually excited to see her. I felt a glimmer of happiness in all of my misery that day, and it gave me the motivation to drive to see her. Her face lit up when she saw me, thanking me for the beautiful flowers. I sat in her office, as I had sat there so many times before, in awe of what a woman she was. So bright, witty, compassionate, loving, and unbelievably giving this woman was. How I longed to become something like her. I had intended to tell her how horrible I was feeling that day, but again, I couldn't fucking get the words out of my mouth. I could not tell her that I wanted to die, that I saw no light for myself anymore. I could not tell her that I had pills in my car that I wanted to take. I could not tell her any of this. I wanted to so very badly, but I swear to you, it is like having superglue on your lips when you cannot get the words out that you feel you need to. The pain is excruciating. So I smiled and listened to her words of advice and let them resonate in my mind for that hour and a half. I left her office feeling better, nowhere near happy, but better. I drove to a parking lot behind a Greek Orthodox Church and parked my car in the corner. I stared out the window for a long, long time, just looking at the gray and dreary sky that was above, watching the birds as they flew, and thinking about how badly I wanted to feel better. Eileen's words stuck with me that night, and I am still unsure as to why, but they did. I know how much work and effort she had put into trying to help me, and I felt an overwhelming sense of guilt about the racing thoughts of suicide that felt like fire in my mind. I started at the Percocet I had with me, prescribed with intent to help me bear the pain of the miscarriage, and I thought nothing could help me anymore. I didn't even feel physical pain; all I felt was emotional heaviness. I cut my arms wide open to try and feel something that night, to try and tell myself that I was alive, and I did feel things like normal people. But no matter how many cuts I made with a knife on a key chain, I could not feel them. It was then that I held the Percocet bottle up to my mouth, began to dump the contents into my mouth, and stopped at three pills when I heard Eileen's voice telling me that I would have a future someday. I dropped the bottle and called her. I asked for her help, and I sobbed my way through giving her directions on where to find me.

She came, got in the car and yelled at me, and I knew I deserved it. I remember an ambulance, and people asking me way too many fucking questions. I remember hugging her and feeling her hold me while lights flashed and people spoke and feeling for once a sense of calm in my destructing world. I got into the ambulance and watched the cars drive by on the highway. I was still wishing I was somebody else, living somebody else's life. I looked at the cuts on my arm I had made and knew that these represented a whole different class of emotions. These represented absolute desperation.

I was wheeled into a room in the Bridgeport Hospital psych ward that was bright blue. So bright in fact that it required you to squint. Was this their attempt at trying to make a depressed person happy? Or trying to force out all negative emotions while in this room with painfully bright paint? I have no idea why the room was such a horrifying color, but I know that I absolutely hated it. I hated that I was still alive, and I hated myself for dragging Eileen here with me to this ugly room. I hated everything about everything. I sat there, answering all the routine questions that they always ask in the emergency room, getting angrier every second. I wanted to scream, *Just fucking kill me.* But instead of course, I just answered the questions like I was supposed to. I was itching to get out of that place. All I wanted to do was bash my head against a wall, run far, far away from all of this hospital stuff, and lie in a bed of misery forever. But that was an impossible task now, as I lay there under the supervision of about five staff and a camera. I have never wanted to just disappear so badly as I did those two days in that fucking blue room.

And three weeks later, I am sitting on my bedroom floor, sobbing after an argument with my parents about the fact that I would rather kill myself than live. It's like no one can even validate the fact that I am in such distress that I feel I can no longer hang on. It's almost like no one really wants to believe that I *am* this depressed, and I am suicidal. Every time I try to communicate such feelings of holy terror, I get shut down with the fact that my illness is treatable and there are medications that can help and that I don't *really* want to die, I just don't want to live in the real world. Well, all this treatment and all this psychodynamic bullshit doesn't seem to help me much when I am sitting on my floor, getting the words out on paper that I cannot push out of my mouth. It's really wonderful when it's New Year's Eve and you don't want the new year to even come because you are convinced that it's just going to be another big disappointment full of sorrow. It's really wonderful when you are wiping your snot and drying your eyes while the rest of the world gets ready to celebrate that it's a new beginning and a new year. What about the people who just want to go back in time and erase it all and just start over from there? What about the people who cannot move on from 2009 and just have a fresh start because they are trapped inside of themselves? What about the people who are desperate and screaming for help? Are they going to get it in 2010? Is it going to be the magical year of recovery? I don't even care anymore. I am apathetic to a new year and a fresh start. I have tried that time and time again, and I end up feeling the same feelings year after year. Maybe if I had read this to my therapist three weeks ago, I would be getting help. Or maybe I would be sitting here, because people seem to think all I want to do is run away like a big baby when life gets too hard. But do they understand that it's either running away to a hospital or it's running away from my life? No. They don't understand it. I love my therapist, and I wish to *God* that I could tell her all of these things, but I don't fucking know why I cannot get them out of my goddamn mouth when I sit in her office. I don't just want to go live in a hospital where people take care of my every need. I don't want to be babied into recovery. I don't want Chicago be my baby blanket. But how am I supposed to feel when I know that it's either I run somewhere where there is safety and comfort, or I run the opposite direction into a place I have only been able to imagine at this point? Maybe if I didn't get out of bed for weeks, or I attempted to overdose more than one time, or if I went down to ninety-four pounds again, then it would be acceptable for me to run to a place where safety lies. But until then, I am sitting here on my carpet waiting for someone to hear me. Then someone suggests I am upset because it is New Year's Eve and I am alone and this what is making me upset. Um, no. It is not fucking because it's New Year's Eve and I am alone. I feel this way day in and day out, and there is no escape from it. It consumes me. I am one with my illness right now and can radically fucking accept that I am one with bipolar. Bifuckingpolar. And dialectical behavioral therapy is supposed to help me. I am supposed to use my coping mechanisms and distract myself from all of this madness that surrounds me. So I take a hot shower and try to redirect my mind. But all I can think about in the hot shower is how I want to get out and go back to my curled-up fetal position in my room. I want to open the blades to my razor and rip open my skin again. I want to feel anything but this darkness that I feel. My grandmother comes over, and we have pizza and salad and a fire and wine, and it's all so wonderful from the outside looking in. I know I should be grateful for all of the things I have and the people who are willing to support me, but all I can think is that I am exhausted already and

I have been out in my living room for five minutes. I am exhausted from fighting this overwhelming shadow of absolute nothingness so that I can be the Amanda everyone knows and loves for at least an hour. Just a goddamn hour. Please won't you let me feel *something* for an hour? Let me feel the warmth of my grandmother's heart or the taste of coffee on my lips. Let me feel the love, the joy, the strength that my grandmother possesses. Please God, please let me feel this. My depression consumes my mind, and I cannot feel these things as I once did. I feel so fucking trapped that I just want to end this suffering. People keep telling me to take it one minute at a time, but I can't tell you what it feels like to be on the edge of a cliff that is depression and the cliff is crumbling underneath you. These illusions and descriptions are not merely for the purpose of writing. They are real to me, and I see them play them throughout my mind all day long. These illusions are my reality, and that fact is dreadfully terrifying. But still, another night passes, and I am still alive. I am still fucking alive.

Last night was New Year's Eve. While all my family got together and ate and drank and was merry, I was home in my room on my floor, crying and screaming to my parents that I didn't want to live anymore. I rang in the New Year in a Seroquel coma. Some party I was at. All night long I wished to God that I could just feel well enough to get to my aunt's house. I prayed for the motivation to actually get up and move so that I could physically just get there. If I could just *get* there, I wouldn't be so miserable. But depression won again, and I sat on my floor and screamed. I wanted nothing more than to be celebrating with my friends, like any twenty-year-old would want to be doing. I wanted to kiss someone at midnight and get drunk on champagne and stay up making resolutions with people that I barely know. I want nothing more in this world than to feel normal. And for some goddamn reason, I just can't feel anything but numb. And after all that has gone on in the past few months, the only person who crossed my mind last night was John. I just wanted to wish away the past four months of my life and be wrapped up in him this New Year's Eve. But I couldn't, and I'm just sitting wishing for things that will never be. Happy fucking New Year to me.

There is no explanation for the madness of racing thoughts throughout your mind. There is no way to ever accurately describe what it feels like to never be able to shut your mind off. Fuck, it just never goes away.

So now I am in DBT. Dialectical Behavioral Therapy. I am learning new ways to cope with life and urges and this and that. I just sit in that classroom day in and day out wondering when the hell I am actually going to be able to pull it together enough to actually *really* use these skills. When am I going to decide that purging is not an option for me? When will I decide that cutting my skin open to the point where I need stitches is not effective? Most of the time I don't know when the time is going to come where I pull it together and get on with my life. Actually, most of the time I don't even want to pull it together.

A few weeks ago, I took fifty Tylenol. Sitting in my car in the church parking lot at the end of my street, I gave in to the voices that torment my mind. I just took handful after handful and silenced them for at least a few minutes. I stared at the church and cursed God; I glanced at my scarred arms and legs and cursed myself. I called Eileen—I cried for help. I called Cindy and cried for forgiveness. She stayed on the phone with me until I got myself to the emergency room and asked to talk to the first nurse I saw. It was Jane Packer, the mother of one of my best high school friends. I sobbed at the sight of her and thought to myself, *what has my life become?* I saw Phoebe working in the ER when I walked through to my room. She was so painfully thin, and I became jealous. Fuck, why could everyone else get away with being sick, and here I am drinking fucking charcoal and throwing up everywhere? Being wheeled up into the ICU, watching my family come and go. People asking me why. *Why?* Who the fuck knows the answer to the question why. God doesn't even have an answer to why. I don't know why I took those pills—I don't even care at this point. I came home from a disastrous stay in the behavioral health unit, which included a roommate telling me she wished she could wrap the cord of the vacuum cleaner the cleaning lady was using around her neck and die right here. My response was "cool." I just needed to get the fuck out of there. Actually, that feeling of needing to get out *right* this instant never leaves me. Everywhere I am I need to be somewhere else. What kind of life is that? Fuck, it's not really a life at all.

    I moved from Silver Hill DBT to Westport DBT in hopes that a more intensive program would help me get it back together again. The honeymoon phase of coming out of the hospital wore off about a week ago. The phase where I say, "How could I really want to die? Life is so worth living and so beautiful." Now I'm right back to Miss Pessimist. I shiver all day long in the sun, I smoke five cigarettes in a row, I avoid eating, I binge and I purge, I am tired, I am manic, I am lonely, I am suffocated, my mind won't shut off, I'm not sleeping, I'm mad at everything, I hate trying so hard, I hate being in treatment, I want to be normal. When I come up for a breath, I think, *I am drowning, and I can't be saved.*

I'm tired of being sick—but I am even more tired of trying so hard and getting nowhere. I don't want to feel like this anymore. I just want to blow lines of coke, shoot heroin, stop eating, take my Seroquel, and sleep all day. I just want to get the fuck out of myself. It is a terrible feeling being twenty—almost twenty-one now—and living at home, not working, and picking the pockets of your parents for therapy. I just want to move on and get on with my life. This disease has me paralyzed, and it captures me and forces me back the minute I try to break free from it. I am wrapped up in the death-tight grip of bipolar again for another round of cycles and ever-changing moods. I lie comatose in my bed with a mind moving faster than the speed of light. I lie in the sun cold as death. I smile on the outside, and I am heaving on the inside. There is no escape from this. This is who I will be my entire life.

CHAPTER NINETEEN

I can't breathe, I can't sleep, I can't eat, and I can't stop purging. I want you back.

I had big plans for us, you know. You were going to be something so amazing to me that I cannot even begin to explain to you what you meant. I freaked out when I saw those two pink lines on that test that afternoon, but deep down my heart fluttered and reset, knowing that you were inside of me, growing off of my very own flesh. I remember the night that your father and I didn't use protection. It was a big mistake indeed, but it brought your life into my own, and I will never regret that night as long as I live.

I remember seeing you on the ultrasound—your tiny, little speck of a self inside me. You were beautiful even then, my love. I shuddered when I saw you for that first time. You were real and living—you were growing inside me—that feeling is something that I will never forget. My first baby, the first life that came to me. Oh God, you were amazing.

I went shopping for you three weeks later, picking out all of the strollers and the crib and the car seat that your perfect little body would lie in when you came into this world. I was convinced you would be a girl, but I could have been wrong. I guess I didn't want you to be anything like your father, and being a boy would surely bring you misery. Your grandparents didn't want you—he didn't want you—but you can rest in peace knowing that your life meant the world to me, and even if no one else on this earth wanted you to come, I would have killed, died, given my all for you. I wanted to name you Madison—or Olivia or Abigail. Madison I liked best though. I imagined you growing up and becoming everything that I would want you to be, beautiful and smart and loving, compassionate, friendly, and giving. You would have been so perfect.

With every ultrasound I saw as you grew bigger and bigger inside me, my heart ached for the day that I would meet you. I saw your heartbeat the day before I lost you. I wanted to reach in and hold you even then, kiss you and tell you how much I loved you.

I planned my future with you in it, imagining all of the time I would spend working hard on getting well for you so that I could make your life a living heaven—instead of a living hell like mine has been.

I felt you in me. I saw my belly start to grow slowly, my breasts getting larger so that I could feed you. I felt you from the day I knew about you. Oh God, how I want you back.

When I started bleeding, I cried. It couldn't be—it just could not be, my love. I drove back from Cindy's that night sobbing, looking down at your life seeping from me. No, no, I just saw your tiny, little perfect heartbeat. No. I can't lose you. No, no, no.

I didn't see you on the ultrasound screen anymore. All I saw was a mess of my womb filled with your blood. They sent us home, home to part from one another.

A Tribute to Madness and Smiles

I lost you at Panera. And I'm sitting here tonight writing in the same place where I saw you leave me. Your perfect little sac of life expelled from my womb into a metal container for you to lie in. I pray to God he took you right then and held you—so that you did not have to feel the cold harshness of that container instead of the warm, nurturing flesh and blood of my cradle for you. Could you hear me cry? Could you even know the pain? I know you had very few brain waves then, but what if those waves knew you were leaving me? Were you sad, scared, and alone? Oh my love, I was devastated. I had to leave you there, in that same container that I looked in just a few minutes ago. I left my baby there. I wanted to say good-bye. I wanted to tell you how much I loved you. But all I could do was fall to the floor and sob.

I didn't deal with your loss until now, and it is months and months later. I can't bear the pain of not feeling you here with me anymore.

I guess it is time for me to say good-bye. But I don't want to say good-bye to you. I just want you back. I want you to be here. You were due on June 24—four days before my birthday. It is March, and I would be swollen with your life by now. I just want to feel you here. I miss you. I love you, and I don't ever want to forget you.

I hate your father with all that I have. But a part of me still loves him because he gave life to you. You are him, and you are me, and you are a product of the love we once shared. His love for you may have never existed, but rest knowing that my love for you will never die.

Come back to me—that is all I wish.

I wonder what you would have looked like. Would you have

had my green eyes—or your father's bright blue ones? Would you be bald like I was when I was a baby?

I wonder what you would have done with your life. I just don't understand why God took you away. You were my life for a few weeks, and your life will never leave me.

You gave me so much strength for those few months. You were a miracle even before you came into this world.

My purging has gotten so out control once again that I am suffocating in my urges. Let's take today, for an example. I have done nothing productive all day except put together my little portfolio of pictures and buy new pillows. Other than that, I have binged and purged six times, and it is 2:52 PM. Hey, bulimia, you're a motherfucking bitch.

This pattern repeats itself over and over throughout my entire life, the pattern of losing control before being able to even see through the fog to try and grasp a lifeline. All of a sudden you are swimming in quicksand, filled with emotions and neverending racing thoughts. I have been home almost a year now from Timberline, and here I sit in my bed on a rainy Saturday in early March, right back in the same place I was last spring. Granted, I was much thinner then and was taking at least a box of laxatives a day and was totally convinced that I would forever be miserable. The biggest difference between then and now is my realization that life does go on after illness, and hope comes in many different forms. I have hope now—I have faith. But why am I still doing this to myself, and why can't I fucking just figure it out and move on? Talking about the baby and the miscarriage and John is supposed to make the symptoms lessen—I have been purging my body in therapy rather than in the toilet bowl for some time. But look at what has happened. Now not only am I purging in every toilet I can find, but I am purging on the side of the road, in the office at DBT, in the bathroom outside therapy. I am purging it all—I just want it all out of me. All of these feelings and these fucking emotions are making me crazy, and the only way to slow it down right now is to purge it out. Get it *the fuck* out.

The DBT that I am doing is wonderful. The skills are so well thought out, and if I could only get myself to follow them, I suppose I would be living a "life worth living," which is the ultimate goal of DBT. I don't really think I'm going to be getting there any time soon, seeing as how I am purging in their little bathroom there at the office. A life worth living is very far from my field of vision at this point in my life—I just want to live and not hate life anymore. Is that too much to ask for?

My mind never shuts the fuck up. I've been lying in this bed for two hours, and my mind is telling me I am lazy little shit who needs to get up and be productive. My mind tells me that Jazzy hates me because I have been purging and sleeping all the time and that I need to take better care of her. Now the reality is that I never get the chance to just lie down and do nothing, and she has been sleeping all day as well. But honestly, I feel so guilty for not walking her that I really could cut myself over it. Insane? Yep.

When does this madness end? Does it ever go away or even just become *bearable* at some point in this life? When will I stop stealing my father's credit card and using it to buy shit to binge on? When will I stop overdrawing my account and costing my parents money to cover my inability to function as a normal human being? Fuck, man, I really fuck some things up big time.

I want to move out and get on with this, but I can't get my fucking head out of the toilet.

I should be happy that I got in to see a psychopharmacologist who has a two-year waiting list. I should be happy that she is brilliant with medications, and I should be relieved that someone is going to make life easier for me. But really, I'm not. I'm not a fan of medication; I never have been. I don't want to medicate with pills and realize that in order for me to be a functional human being for the rest of my life that I have to take these stupid pills and just accept it. I want to self-medicate. I want to drive for hours and hours to somewhere I have never been and sit on the beach and stare up at the moon and listen to the waves. I want to buy a Popsicle from the ice cream truck and watch it melt in the summer heat. I want the sand to get caught in my flip-flops, and I want to run, sprint, fly into the ocean. Let the ocean heal me—let the water reform me and restore my soul. The thought of water is magnificent, the way the ocean restores itself. I wish I had the capacity to do such wondrous work.

Instead, I pop Zyprexa and two Klonopin. Totally not as much fun.

CHAPTER TWENTY

I knew that writing this book wouldn't be easy, and I knew it would take a lot of strength to write about all of the shit that has happened to me, but God, it feels good to get it out for someone else to hear. I hope that my life gets better than it is right now, but I can't predict how it will turn out. I guess I just wanted to let you know—whoever you are, wherever you are—I am here, and we are all here for each other. Whatever illness you have or whatever demons you have romping through your life, we are all the same, and we all know the pain, the most excruciating pain of mental illness, and how quietly it kills. Don't ever give up, my friends. We are the strong and the determined, and we will get better somehow, someday. Just hang on, life is waiting for you.

Life is still waiting for me. It is now late April, and I have just stopped eating altogether. I have lost the desire to even binge and purge. I just don't have the energy anymore. But let me tell you, not eating only makes my mood about forty times worse than it normally is. My depression has taken over once again, and I am irritable and miserable, a nightmare for my parents to live with. I have admitted that I need more help—seeing as how I cannot bring myself to accept my body the way that it is on my own—and will be doing an intensive outpatient at the Institute of Living once again, as I did when I was seventeen. I am dedicated to my treatment now—after weeks of wanting to just give up—because I know I simply cannot continue to live my life in this fashion. Starving and bingeing and purging solves absolutely nothing in the long run, and I refuse to give in to my sickness any longer. I don't want to be miserable like this *anymore.*

Life brings us lessons in the smallest ways sometimes. As I write this, I am watching *The Lion King* with the little girl I am babysitting for and have listened to the song "Hakuna Matata" with a newfound determination. No longer will I let this eating disorder worry me. I want to live my life worry free (which is totally unrealistic), but at least I would like to live my life free of worry about food. I will adopt the "eat to live" philosophy and regain control over my life. I will beat this.

Made in the USA
Middletown, DE
04 June 2017